Contents

Projects:

History

It is generally believed that Chinese potters under the T'ang dynasty (618-906 AD), were the first to make true porcelain and their secret was jealously guarded for centuries.

The first outsider to see the marvels of China's potters was Marco Polo who visited the court of Kublai Khan in 1275. Marco Polo is credited for giving porcelain its name, porcellana which is Italian for cowrie shell. Undoubtedly, Polo returned to Venice with some of these prized porcelains, setting off a frenzy among the nobility to aquire vessels fashioned from this treasured substance. Subsequently, porcelains were imported from China at great expense. Importers were besieged with shipwrecks, pirates, robbers, and warfare.

Porcelain was valued with gold and precious gems. Most early pieces were, in fact, mounted in gold, silver, or bronze to offer protection and to provide jewelry-like settings.

Magical powers were attributed to porcelain. It was professed to ward off certain illnesses and be a protection against poison.

In 1602 the Dutch formed the Dutch East India Trading Company and porcelain became more accessible to European nobility. It has been estimated that between 1602 and 1682 more than three million pieces of Chinese porcelain found their way to Europe via Dutch ships.

Marco Polo's introduction of porcelain to Europe prompted numerous efforts at manufacturing the prized substance. The first European soft paste porcelain (Medici) was made in Florence around 1575. Still this ware was a crude form of porcelain and in no way comparative to Chinese porcelain.

The first European hard paste porcelain is imputed to the alchemist Johann Fredrick Bottger and physicist Ehrenfried Walter Tschirnhaus about 1707. Bottger, imprisoned and ordered to make gold by Augustus the Strong, was united with Tschirnhaus who was interested in the process of making porcelain. Bottger's kiln records show that on January 15, 1708, after a twelve-hour firing, he achieved a white, translucent body. Augustus was elated and the Royal Saxon Porcelain Manufactory in Meissen came into being in 1710.

The next emphasis was on modeling and decorating to the standards of the Chinese and Japanese imports. Joachim Kandler, who worked at the Meissen factory for forty years, is credited with the creation of over a thousand different figures which have been endlessly reproduced. The earliest decoration was copied from Ming and Ch'ing vase painting. Decoration became so sophisticated that Meissen porcelains were taken for Chinese.

Bottger's porcelain formula was closely guarded but it was not long before the secret was out and other countries began producing porcelain. The second true porcelain factory was founded in Vienna around 1719. From Vienna the secret spread through the Rhineland to Russia, Switzerland, Denmark, Italy, Spain, France, and England.

By 1800 Josiah Spode II of England added calcined bones to hard paste porcelain to create bone china which was prized because of its resistance to chipping. The Spode factory is also credited with making the statuary porcelain commonly called Parian ware. Parian is named for Parian marble and is a biscuit porcelain which is vitrified, transparent, and easily molded.

Credit for the first successful American porcelain manufacture goes to William Ellis Tucker of Philadelphia, who found a factory there in 1825. Parian ware was manufactured in the 1850's at Bennington, Vermont, and by 1875 the United States had its own flourishing porcelain industry.

In 1896, Walter Scott Lenox founded Lenox, Inc. in Trenton, New Jersey, which became one of the largest and most important American porcelain companies. Almost from its inception, Lenox produced the china dinnerware for our White House.

The Cybis firm was founded in 1942 by Boleslaw Cybis who wished to create porcelains in the tradition of Europe's old master craftsmen. The factory he founded continues to produce stunning examples of American art porcelain.

Edward Marshall Boehm, who greatly admired Chinese porcelains and professed that, ". . . nothing is technically impossible," worked on porcelain between 1944 and 1949. With only one thousand dollars, he moved to Trenton and began the empire which today is Boehm Porcelains known world over for their magnificent porcelain masterpieces.

Helen Schaeffer

THE JOYS OF PORCELAIN

ISBN #0-916809-18-8
Library of Congrc33 - 87-062048
PRINTED IN U.S.A.
First Printing - July 1987
Second Printing - May 1997
Copyright© 1987 Scott Publications
30595 Eight Mile, Livonia, MI 48152-1798

Scott
PUBLICATIONS

THE JOYS OF PORCELAIN

Dedication

...to the memory of my father, Eugene Walters,

who built my studio, poured my molds, and taught me

that I could do anything I wanted if I would only try

and

...to my husband and best friend, Stan, who

labors by my side, encourages me to do whatever I want

to do, and supports me in all my ventures.

I dedicate this book with love.

— Helen Schaeffer

Introduction

Porcelain has been shrouded in mystery since its discovery. What is this substance, jealously coveted, prized by nobility in the past, and still worthy of being highly valued and prestigious gifts to heads of state today?

Porcelain is a combination of kaolin (and sometimes ball clay), feldspar, and flint which forms a white, vitreous and translucent surface when fired to a high temperature. Porcelain appears more fragile than earthenware or stoneware yet, when fired is very hard and durable. Porcelain is somewhat resonant when struck.

The qualities of whiteness, hardness, and translucency have always made porcelain more esteemed than earthenware. Porcelain is elegant, aristocratic, and admired by all.

Now you are probably thinking, "That's all fine, but where is its place in hobby ceramics? Everyone knows that porcelain is too expensive, much too difficult to work with, and is limited as to what you can do with it."

Nonsense! Read on and you will find that all this is myth. The purpose of this book is to introduce you to the most wonderful, beautiful, and versa-tile tile of clay bodies —porcelain.

My husband and I have had a love affair with porcelain from the beginning of our ceramic careers. Whenever someone told us that an idea for a project was impossible to complete in porcelain, we smiled and set out to prove them wrong. We found that porcelain was suitable for anything and that its limitations were only in the confines of people's minds.

Try this fascinating medium and I guarantee you will realize many hours of enjoyment creating both utilitarian ware and ornamental items destined to become family heirlooms.

Let's begin with the myth that porcelain is expensive. Yes, a gallon of porcelain slip does cost more than a gallon of earthenware slip. However, a gallon of porcelain goes a long way. Castings are thinner and therefore you will get more castings per gallon of slip. In addition, the wear and tear on molds is negligible compared to that caused by earthenware. If you already have some molds, they can be cleaned and used for casting porcelain.

Again and again I hear all sorts of reasons why porcelain is difficult to work with. All I can say is that if you follow the simple step-by-step directions in this book you will be turning out creations that you will be justly proud of and be the envy of your friends.

What are the limitations of this majestic clay body? Virtually none. Fine translucent bud vases, to bold, heavier cast lamp bases, to those magnificent reproduction dolls, to utilitarian teapots are all within the realm of this wonderful clay. Glazed or unglazed, carved or cutout, finished in underglaze or overglaze virtually anything is possible.

Within these pages you will find directions for casting, cleaning, firing, and techniques for everything from underglaze brushwork to china painted dolls. All I can say is: give it a try — you'll be very happy you did!

Choosing a Mold:

When selecting a mold to be cast in porcelain, choose only one with good, clean details. This is no time to use a worn and pitted mold. Some folks will tell you that you can't cast porcelain in a mold that has been used for low-fire pottery castings. This is not true. It is necessary to thoroughly clean the mold or molds you intend to pour if they were previously used to cast other clays. Molds discolored from other clays may be cleaned by wiping them with a sponge or

cotton ball dampened with alcohol.

We are fortunate to have a multitude of porcelain slips available to us today. Porcelain slip is attainable not only in various tones of white but also in virtually every color and even in black. Different colored slips from the same manufacturer may be mixed to obtain other colors, so that you can be assured of finding the perfect slip color for a special project.

Preparation of Slip:

Since porcelain slips are made by several manufacturers, each one may pour and handle a little differently. You will soon learn the characteristics of the slip you are working with. If one slip is not to your liking, try another.

Essential to the casting process is the proper preparation of the slip. It is imperative that adequate time be allocated to stirring the slip. I find that slip cannot be thoroughly stirred in the container in which it was purchased. Instead, pour the slip into a large, rustproof container or bucket. A long wooden-handled rubber spatula works well for stirring. There are also slip mixers which can be attached to a drill motor. The slip must be adequately mixed to a smooth, free-flowing, creamy consis-

tency; however, care must be taken not to whip air into the slip, as air bubbles will cause pin holes in the castings. If the slip remains too heavy, the addition *of a very small* amount of water will bring it to the proper consistency. It is a good idea to strain the slip through a rustproof strainer to remove any lumps or bits of dried porcelain clay.

Casting:

Begin with a clean, tightly banded mold. Slowly and steadily pour the slip into the mold. Too slow a pour will cause rings to form in the clay (hesitation marks), while a very rapid pour will trap air and cause bubbles in the casting. Fill the mold completely to the top. Some molds will have to be topped off with additional slip several times as the slip level recedes.

How long should the slip remain in the mold before draining? There is no one easy answer to this question. Many things influence set-up time. You may find that a small bud vase will setup in one minute, while a large lamp base (which you would naturally want heavier for durability), might take much longer. Different casting slips have different set-up times. Set up is also influenced by the dryness of the mold, room temperature, and humidity. The answer to this dilemma is to

watch the casting as it builds up at the pour hole and drain the mold when it has reached the desired thickness.

To drain the mold, slowly and continuously empty the remaining slip back into the container. Too rapid a draining can create a vacuum which could cause the casting to pull away from the side of the mold or cause it to collapse.

It is a good idea to reverse the angle of the mold several times while draining to prevent slip from puddling on one side of the casting. After draining completely, allow the mold to remain upside down, propped up to permit air to circulate. This will allow the casting to dry uniformly.

Trouble may be encountered when casting porcelain due to the rapid in-mold shrinkage of the casting. This shrinking in the mold can cause the casting to crack. Two things will help prevent this problem. First, remove the spare (if possible) from the pour hole as soon as the casting is no longer dripping; this takes some of the stress off of the casting. Never, never tear off the spare as this will put more stress on the casting and the ragged edge thus produced may be responsible for stress crack which will not show up until after the ware is fired. Always remove the spare with a sharp fettling knife. There are some molds which must be opened before the spare can be removed.

The other important step in casting is to open the mold as soon as it will release. If the mold will not open, do not force it; rather, continue to try to open the mold at intervals until it opens easily. Forcing the mold could rip the casting or at least cause warping. Porcelain has a "memory" and once warping occurs, it cannot be undone. Even though you carefully restore a warped piece while the clay is still soft, memory will cause the piece to distort again during the firing.

Mention should be made here about wearing rings and other jewelry, having long fingernails, and using hand creams when pouring and handling porcelain.

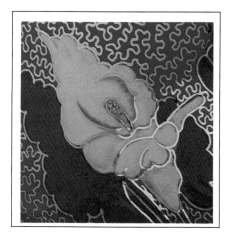

Firing:

A pre-requisite of firing porcelain is an absolutely clean kiln. Vacuum the kiln on a regular basis to prevent contamination of the ware by rust and other impurities. Keep in mind that any glaze drips left on shelves will stick to the ware and ruin it. Good housekeeping will pay off when working with porcelain.

Clean, freshly kiln washed shelves are another necessity for good ware. Apply high-fire kiln wash to only the top side of each shelf.

A thin (a dusting) of hydrated alumina or fine silica sand on the shelves will allow the porcelain ware to move easily as it shrinks during firing.

Porcelain demands special firing procedures because of the degree of softening which takes place in the clay during the high maturing temperature required. If you were able to reach inside the kiln when the porcelain reaches its maturation temperature, the ware would be as soft as a ball of clay.

A long and slow firing is best for porcelain. Here again, you must be familiar with the brand of porcelain you are using. The temperature at which various porcelain clays mature differ somewhat. The majority of commercial porcelain slips available to the hobby ceramist, mature at cone 5 or cone 6.

It is advisable to follow the written instructions for your particular kiln. All kiln instruction booklets contain information on porcelain firing. The schedule my husband and I have always used is as follows:

Pre-fire: 2 hours low setting; lid cracked; peep holes open.

Fire: 2 hours low setting; lid closed; bottom peep holes closed; top peep hole open.

Fire: 3 hours medium setting; lid closed; bottom peep holes closed; top peep hole open.

Then turn to high until the automatic shutoff operates.

Following this schedule, a load of porcelain fires in 8 to 12 hours, depending on the amount of ware

Jewelry and fingernails can cause dents or other gouges in the soft clay. Hand cream will seal the surface of the ware and cause discoloration or a surface will not accept color.

Attachments or stick-ons may be done either when the ware is leather-hard or when it is dry. My preference is to attach all stick-ons when the porcelain is at the leather-hard stage. Sometimes it is best to score the areas on the ware where a join is to be made. If drying has begun, rewet both areas, then use a soft brush to apply slightly thickened porcelain slip to both the ware and to the stick-on. Firmly position the stick-on onto the ware. You can almost feel a ''grabbing'' when the two pieces meet. Hold the stick-on in place momentarily and then, if any areas remain which could be filled in, do so with additional slip.

Cleaning Porcelain Greenware:

The cast greenware is very fragile. Many people prefer to fire porcelain to cone 018 to strengthen it before cleaning. My preference is to work on porcelain greenware as soon as the casting is thoroughly dry.

Good cleaning is essential for flawless, unblemished bisque. Remember, that the glaze, china paint, or any other finish will tend to reveal rather than conceal any flaws in the surface of the ware.

Cleaning is generally done when the greenware is thoroughly dry. However, some projects, which require numerous stick-ons, are easier accomplished if the stick-ons are cleaned before they are attached. A damp brush works well to clean most attachments.

On dry porcelain greenware, begin by using a sharp cleaning tool to carefully remove the raised seam lines created by the sections of the molds coming together. Use nylon stocking material or a soft nylon net material in a circular motion over the seam areas to further smooth them. Be careful not to remove any details during this process. A dry, semi-soft bristle brush is good for cleaning hard-to-reach areas.

Good lighting will help you to see flaws which may otherwise go unnoticed. Before firing, a final smoothing with a cotton ball is helpful.

The use of water in cleaning porcelain is controversial. Water should never be used on a doll face, and excessive water can cause the loss of detail and may also produce a shiny or textured surface after firing. A damp sponge is helpful in smoothing pour-hole areas.

firing. Fortunately, this phenomena is easily remedied; simply refire the bisque to a true cone 6.

Overfiring — Overfired porcelain usually appears shiny and may also blister. Sadly, there is no way of salvaging these pieces. A word to the wise — don't rely entirely upon your automatic firing device use witness cones to assure proper temperature.

Glazing:

It is important to find a glaze that "fits" the body of the porcelain you are using. There are many high-fire glazes available. Most hobby ceramic glazes will fire to cone 4 or cone 6. The glazes in the red family will not high fire. Run a test or check with the manufacturer to be certain before you ruin a great project.

Because porcelain bisque is a vitrified body, glaze takes much longer to dry. It is helpful to warm the bisque in a 150 degree oven for a few minutes before applying the glaze. When brushing glaze, use a damp, fully-loaded glaze mop to flow the glaze onto the bisque. If you work the brush back and forth, it will pull the glaze. Do not apply glaze too heavily. Drips and runs are easy to sand off with a rubber scrubber after they have dried.

Spraying the glaze is the preferred method of application for many porcelain artists. This allows for even coverage. Thin coverage is best. You can always reglaze, but you can't remove unsightly, fired glaze drips.

All glazed pieces must be dry footed to prevent them from sticking to the kiln shelves during firing. Stilts cannot be used because at the high temperature necessary to mature the glaze (usually 2 "cones" lower than for the bisque fire), they would become embedded into the porcelain.

and shelves in the load. It is advisable that you develop the habit of using witness cones to check on the automatic control and so avoid the special problems mentioned below.

Leave the lid closed until the kiln is completely cool to the touch. A good rule of thumb is to allow the kiln to cool the same length of time as the firing. Therefore, if the firing took ten hours, you should plan on allowing the kiln to cool down for ten hours before you open it.

When loading porcelain for the bisque firing, some precautions must be taken. Porcelain pieces may not touch during this firing or they will adhere to one another. In spite of this, boxes must be fired with their lids in place to assure good fit. To prevent the lids from adhering permanently, paint the rims that touch with either high-fire kiln wash (diluted with water) or hydrated alumina (mixed with water to a milk-like consistency). A light coat of either material will work well as a separator.

When firing large, unbalanced or top heavy pieces, it is necessary to prop overhanging heavy areas, which would otherwise sag during the firing. Porcelain shrinks (up to 15% depending on the porcelain), therefore the props must be fashioned from the same unfired porcelain as the piece to be fired, so that both piece and prop will shrink at the same rate.

Save the spares and trimmings when you cast porcelain, add a bit of plasticizer to them and roll coils to use for props. Use a lace tool to prick holes through the props to allow for the release of trapped air.

It will save much frustration to assemble and prop difficult pieces directly on the kiln shelf before placing the shelf in the kiln.

In recent years, a new porcelain propping material has become available. This prop is a non-asbestos fiber which resembles cotton and is placed under any area needing propping in order to prevent sagging. Some special problems may be encountered when firing dolls. When firing doll heads, place the greenware heads in the kiln on a 1/8" to 1/4" layer of hydrated alumina. Breastplates retain their shapes well if fired upside down, and closed dome heads are successfully fired when the top of the head is placed in a bed of hydrated alumina.

Firing Problems:

Underfiring — Underfired porcelain has a chalky appearance. Occasionally the porcelain bisque looks mature but, when china painted and fired, appears to have a "mildew" surface. This looks like hundreds of tiny black specks which develop only after the china

Glazing Problems:

Crazing — A glaze which is incompatible with the porcelain will craze. Cooling or opening the kiln too quickly can also cause crazing. Sometimes this problem can be corrected by adding another coat of glaze and refiring.

Grainy glaze — Insufficient glaze will give the ware a grainy feeling. Add another coat of glaze and refire to remedy this problem.

Methods of Decoration:

Virtually any medium can be used to decorate porcelain. The projects found within the pages of this book use a multitude of mediums and techniques.

Translucent Underglaze Colors — These highly concentrated colors are perfect for brushwork designs on porcelain. Beautiful shading techniques can be accomplished with these colors and they are also the best medium for stenciling projects. Most of these colors will fire to cone 6, but a few will change color or fire out. If you are not sure how the translucent underglaze colors you are using will react at high temperatures, it would be wise to run a test porcelain firing

before attempting an important piece.

Underglaze Colors —Three coat-underglaze coverage can be used on porcelain; however, many colors will change at cone 6. Most underglaze colors (because of their clay content) will vitrify at high temperatures. Regardless of this, they have their place in porcelain decoration.

Glazes — There are many good high-fire glazes available. Additionally, most hobby ceramic glazes are capable of being fired to high temperatures. Satin and dull matte glazes will tend to become glossy. Glazes in the red family will fire out. First, consult the manufacturer's literature, then run glaze test fires to be assured that the glaze selected is compatible with the clay body. Some stand-up-type glazes can be successfully fired to cone 6. Again, if unsure, run a test fire.

Overglazes — An overglaze is a low-fired material used over a fired glaze. Because porcelain is vitreous, it is possible to put the overglaze directly onto the bisque. Before doing so, it is important to smooth the bisque with a #220 grit scrubber. In the case of dolls, this is an extremely important step. Any rough areas left on the bisque tend to "grab" the color and give the painting a blotchy appearance; therefore, special attention must be given to any hard-to-reach areas.

China Paint — Most ceramists think of china paint for decorating porcelain. Of course it is the medium of choice for reproduction dollmaking. China paint can be used directly on the bisque or over a glaze, depending on the desired results. China paints are available as dry powders or premixed, moist colors. There are several different types of mediums available for use with china paints. China painted pieces are generally fired between thin applications of color.

Fired Metallics — Don't overlook fired metallics as the sole decorating medium as in the elegantly simple "Shimmering Pagodas" project found elsewhere in this book. Fired metallics may be used on glazed or unglazed porcelain. On unglazed porcelain, the effect will be that of burnished metal.

Enamel-type Glazes — Several manufacturers produce these lovely and intriguing glazes. The firing range is from cone 018 to cone 05. For porcelain techniques, I use these colors as overglazes and fire them to cone 018 to simulate the beautiful Oriental enamel designs.

Petroleum-base Translucent Stain —This medium is especially suited for porcelain figurines, as its translucent property allows the beauty of the porcelain to show through, retaining the delicate quality of the clay. Most manufacturers have an oil medium available to use with their stains. The medium allows these colors to be blended with unbelievable realism.

Blue and White Stencil Design

Technique: Stenciling

The inspiration for this vase came from a porcelain coffeepot made between 1740 and 1745 at Doccia, near Florence, Italy, and decorated with a stenciled floral design. Stenciling is an easy and fun way to decorate porcelain ware.

MATERIALS NEEDED FOR THIS PROJECT:

- [ ] Suitable mold.
- [ ] White porcelain slip.
- [ ] Wedgwood Blue porcelain slip.
- [ ] Cleaning tool.
- [ ] Nylon stocking material.
- [ ] White translucent underglaze color.
- [ ] Glazed tile and palette knife.
- [ ] Stencil.
- [ ] Silk sponge.
- [ ] Glaze brush.
- [ ] High-fire gloss glaze.
- [ ] Liquid bright gold.
- [ ] Pen reserved for gold.

Step 1 — Stir both the white and the Wedgwood Blue porcelain slips. Pour the mold with the Wedgwood Blue slip and allow it to set up one minute, then drain the mold. Refill the mold with the white porcelain slip and allow it to remain until the casting is the desired thickness, then drain.

Step 2 — When the mold can be opened, trim the spare and gently remove the casting.

Step 3 — Allow the greenware vase to dry, then carefully clean it.

Step 4 — Trace the pattern given here onto fairly heavy paper and use a sharp craft knife or a small, sharp scissors to cut out the design.

Step 5 — Condition some White translucent underglaze color on a glazed tile, then pick up a small amount of it on a silk sponge. Holding the stencil firmly in place on the greenware, use the sponge to pounce the color onto the piece through the openings.

Step 6 — Fire the vase to cone 6.

Step 7 — Apply 2 smooth coats of high-fire clear gloss glaze to the inside and outside of the vase. Allow the piece to dry, then fire it to the temperature recommended by the glaze manufacturer.

Using a pen reserved for gold, outline the entire design with liquid bright gold.

Fire the vase to cone 018.

HELEN SCHAEFFER

Wedgwood

Surely you have from time to time admired beautiful and delicate English Wedgwood pieces. Although the technique described here is not exactly identical to the method of production of this lovely English porcelain ware, I'm certain you will find that this reproduction will make you justifiably proud to say, "I made it myself!"

While the following directions call for using blue, the project can be done with any desired color of porcelain slip. Wedgwoodware is generally left unglazed. Remember, porcelain bisque is vitreous and a glaze is not necessary to make the finished piece utilitarian. Should you prefer a glaze, apply two smooth coats of high-fire clear gloss glaze to the bisque and fire to the temperature recommended by the glaze manufacturer.

MATERIALS NEEDED FOR THIS PROJECT

- ☐ Suitable mold.
- ☐ White porcelain slip.
- ☐ Wedgwood Blue porcelain slip.
- ☐ Silk sponge.
- ☐ Flannel material.
- ☐ Cleaning tools.
- ☐ Nylon stocking material.
- ☐ #4 or #6 round brush.

Step 1 — Select a mold which produces greenware with an embossed design and use a wet silk sponge to dampen the design area on one section (this prevents the slip to be applied to the design area from drying too quickly and cracking in the mold or pulling away from the main body of the casting).

Step 2 — Place a small amount of well-stirred white porcelain slip into a small saucer or bowl. Use a damp #4 or #6 round brush (depending on the size of the design in your particular mold) to carefully paint the design with the slip. Start at the outer edges and work toward the center of the design. Add enough layers of white porcelain slip to completely fill the design area of the mold. When the design is filled, cover the design area with a piece of damp flannel material while you work on another section of the mold.

Repeat the procedure for the other half of the mold.

Step 3 — Remove the flannel material, put the mold parts together, and tightly band. Pour the mold with Wedgwood Blue slip, completely filling it. Allow the slip to remain in the mold until the casting reaches the proper thickness, then drain the mold.

Step 4 — When the casting is sufficiently dry, remove the spare, open the mold, and gently remove the vase.

Step 5 — Allow the vase to dry thoroughly, then remove the seam lines and smooth the neck. Take care so as not to contaminate the white design with the blue porcelain dust.

Step 6 — Fire to cone 6.

The Holy Family

Technique — Regular underglaze colors

This technique uses regular underglaze colors to mimic the famous porcelains of Spain. Before starting this project, it would be wise to test fire the underglaze colors you are planning to use, since some underglaze colors can show a marked change when fired to high temperatures.

MATERIALS NEEDED FOR THIS PROJECT
☐ Suitable molds.
☐ White porcelain slip.
☐ Cleaning tools.
☐ Nylon stocking material.
☐ Glazed tile and palette knife.
☐ Regular underglaze colors — Flesh, Madonna Blue, Peat Brown, Almond, Primitive, Wedgwood, and Smoke Gray.
☐ Translucent underglaze colors — Pink, Rawhide, Cinnamon, and Lampblack.
☐ Copenhagen glaze.
☐ Brushes — #4 and #6 round, detail, and glaze mop.

Step 1 — Pour the molds for the figurines with White porcelain slip. When you remove the pieces from the molds, use slip to attach the birds in the proper places on the Baby and on Mary's knee. Do not attach the lamb at this time.

Step 2 — Allow the greenware to dry, then carefully clean all of the pieces.

Step 3 — Using the round brushes, apply 3 smooth coats of the following underglaze colors to the indicated areas.
Flesh — Faces, arms, and feet.
Madonna Blue — Mary's veil.
Smoke Gray — All bases.
Peat Brown — Joseph's robe.
Primitive — Manger and Joseph's staff.
Almond — Straw.
Wedgwood — Birds.

Step 4 — Condition the translucent underglaze colors to creamy consistencies on a glazed tile, then use a detail brush to apply them as follows: Rawhide, Mary's and the Baby's hair and eyebrows.
Cinnamon, Joseph's hair and eyebrows and all sandals.
Pink, lips.
Lampblack — Eye details on figures, lamb, and birds.

Step 5 — Fire all of the pieces to cone 6.

Step 6 — Apply 2 flowing coats of Copenhagen glaze to each piece. Dryfoot all pieces. Position the lamb beside the manger so that it is looking up at the Baby.

Fire to the temperature recommended by the glaze manufacturer.

Oriental Simplicity

Technique — Sgraffito of double-cast ware

Sometimes a very simple design can be quite elegant, as in this double-cast vase with its modest sgraffitoed plum blossom design. Double casting porcelain is rewarding and this easy project is an excellent introduction to the technique.

MATERIALS NEEDED FOR THIS PROJECT
☐ Suitable mold.
☐ Wedgwood Blue porcelain slip.
☐ White porcelain slip.
☐ Sgraffito tools.
☐ Cleaning tools.
☐ Nylon stocking material.
☐ Soft brush.

Step 1 — Select, clean, and band a suitable mold.

Thoroughly stir both the Wedgwood Blue and the White porcelain slips. Pour the mold with the Wedgwood Blue slip and allow it to set up for about two minutes — no more! Drain the mold and immediately refill it with the well-stirred White porcelain slip. Allow this slip to remain in the mold until the casting has attained the desired thickness. Drain the mold and, when the casting is very firm, remove the spare and open the mold. Carefully remove the casting.

Step 2 — When the greenware has dried to the leather-hard stage, make a tracing of the design given here and transfer it to the piece or sketch it on. It is not necessary to use carbon paper if you trace the design, simply use just enough pressure on the pencil to make slight indentations into the greenware.

Use any of the numerous sgraffito tools available — those with round cutting edges, oval shapes, or the type which merely cut lines of varying widths.

Begin with the round petals of the design and sgraffito through the Blue porcelain to expose the White beneath it (I used a round, scoop-type sgraffito tool). Scoop out the oval design next, then do the line work (I used an oval-shaped scoop for the oval portions of the design and several sizes of regular sgraffito tools for the lines). When working on the lines, remember that to avoid chipping the design it is best not to cross existing sgraffitoed lines; rather, cut away from them.

Allow the vase to dry thoroughly.

Step 3 — Use nylon stocking material to gently remove the seam lines and to smooth out the rim of the vase, holding the piece upside down, so that the blue porcelain dust does not fall into it. Use a soft brush to smooth out any sgraffito areas which may be rough.

Step 4 — Fire to cone 6.

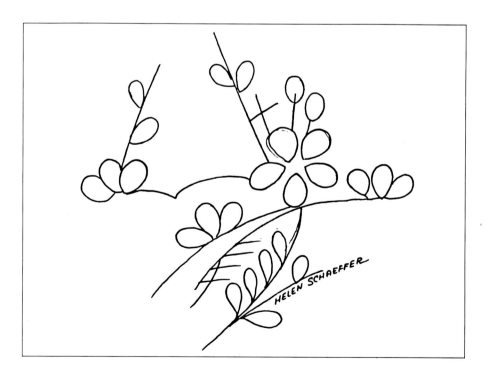

Carved Daisy in Blue

Technique — Carving double-cast ware

This project is another adventure in double casting. Whereas in the first double-cast project we used sgraffito tools, for this one we will use a sharp knife to cut through one color of porcelain to expose the other beneath it. Once you have tried this method of carving double-cast ware you will use it again and again, since variations are endless.

MATERIALS NEEDED FOR THIS PROJECT

- ☐ Suitable mold.
- ☐ Azure porcelain slip.
- ☐ White porcelain slip.
- ☐ Pure talc.
- ☐ Sharp knife.
- ☐ Cleaning tools.
- ☐ Nylon stocking material.
- ☐ Soft brush.
- ☐ High-fire kiln wash.
- ☐ Clear gloss glaze.
- ☐ Brushes — Glaze mop, stiff bristle, and brush reserved for gold.
- ☐ Liquid bright gold.

Step 1 — Tightly band a cleaned mold.

Thoroughly stir both the Azure and White porcelain slips, making sure that they are both free of lumps.

Step 2 — Pour the lid mold with White porcelain slip and allow it to set up for only a minute, then drain it back into the pouring container. As soon as the shine has disappeared from the casting in the mold, very lightly dust the inside of it with talc (the talc will enable you to easily lift out the cut sections of the design). Immediately refill the lid mold with Azure porcelain slip and allow it to set up until the desired thickness is achieved, then drain the mold. Pour the mold for the box section in just Azure slip.

Step 3 — As soon as the lid mold can easily be opened, gently remove the casting.

Step 4 — Carefully sketch or trace the design onto the top of the egg box lid.

Step 5 — Use a sharp, narrow-bladed knife to delicately cut through the White layer of porcelain along the design outlines. Gently remove the cutout areas to expose the Azure porcelain. Cut the entire design in this manner.

Step 6 — Allow the box and lid to dry thoroughly, then use nylon stocking material to carefully smooth out the rims of both pieces. Smooth any rough areas of the design edges with a soft brush.

Step 7 — Apply a liberal coat of high-fire kiln wash to the rim of each piece.

Step 8 — With the lid in place, fire the box to cone 6.

Step 9 — Use a stiff brush to remove any traces of kiln wash from the rims. Apply 2 smooth coats of clear glaze to the inside and outside of each piece. Dryfoot the box and lid and fire them to the temperature recommended by the glaze manufacturer.

Step 10 — Using a brush reserved for gold, apply liquid bright gold to the cut edges of the design on the lid.

Fire the lid to cone 018.

Hearts and Flowers

Technique — Translucent underglaze, brushwork, and specialty glaze

This project features a simple yet romantic design on which to practice your brushstrokes. The stand-up-type specialty glaze makes the heart especially attractive.

MATERIALS NEEDED FOR THIS PROJECT
☐ Suitable Pink porcelain greenware.
☐ Cleaning tools.
☐ Nylon stocking material.
☐ Glazed tile and palette knife.
☐ Translucent underglaze colors — White, Pink Lady, Cranberry, Heavenly Blue, Lemon Drop, Green Grape, and Spruce Green.
☐ Glazes — Stand-up-type specialty and clear gloss.
☐ Brushes — #4 round, #2 liner, #8 square shader, glaze mop, and brush reserved for gold.
☐ Liquid bright gold.
☐ High-fire kiln wash.

Step 1 — Pour the heart box molds with Pink porcelain slip. Remove the castings and allow them to dry thoroughly.

Step 2 — Carefully clean the porcelain greenware, making sure that the lid fits the box correctly.

Step 3 — Place some of each translucent underglaze color in a separate spot on a glazed tile and condition it with water to a creamy consistency.

Apply the colors to the indicated areas:

Roses — Use the #4 round brush to fill in the bowl and petals of the roses with Lady Pink.

Shade each rose along the outer portion of the petals and the top of the bowl with Cranberry.

Leaves — Fill in the leaves with Green Grape, then shade the bottom of each one with Spruce Green, using a side-loaded #8 square shader brush. Paint the veins on the leaves with Spruce Green.

Small flowers — For these flowers, use the #4 round brush and Heavenly Blue to make tiny pressure strokes, then paint the centers with Lemon Drop.

Ribbon — Paint the ribbon with White.

Step 5 — Side load a #8 square shader brush with White and shade around each scallop surrounding the inner heart.

Step 6 — Use a pointed brush handle to apply dots of stand-up-glaze around the entire outside of the scallop design and to the centers of the roses and the small blue flowers.

Step 7 — Apply a liberal coat of high-fire kiln wash to the rim of the lid and the heart box.

Step 8 — Fire the box with the lid in place to cone 6.

Step 9 — Remove all traces of kiln wash from the pieces. Use a glaze mop to apply 2 coats of high-fire gloss glaze to the inside and outside of the box and lid. Dryfoot both pieces, then fire them to the maturing temperature of the glaze.

Step 10 — Using a brush reserved for gold, outline and detail the ribbon and the scallops on the heart box lid.

Step 11 — Fire the lid to cone 018.

21

Stenciled Flowers

Technique — Stenciling

Everyone seems to be stenciling these days — everything from fabrics, to walls, to floors. Here's a stencil project for porcelain which is fast, simple, and fun.

MATERIALS NEEDED FOR THIS PROJECT
- [ ] Suitable white porcelain greenware.
- [ ] Cleaning tools.
- [ ] Nylon stocking material.
- [ ] Glazed tile and palette knife.
- [ ] Silk sponge.
- [ ] Translucent underglaze colors — Pink Lady, Maize, Heavenly Blue, and Green Grape.
- [ ] Heavy paper.
- [ ] Craft knife or small, sharp scissors.
- [ ] Glaze mop brush.
- [ ] High-fire clear gloss glaze.
- [ ] Liquid bright gold.
- [ ] Pen for gold.

Step 1 — Pour the molds with white porcelain slip. Remove the castings and allow them to dry.

Step 2 — Carefully clean the greenware and drill a drainage hole in the bottom of the planter.

Step 3 — Trace the pattern onto fairly heavy paper. Use a sharp craft knife or a small, sharp scissors to cut out only the sections which will be green leaves. Spray the stencil with an aerosol fixative to make it more durable.

Step 4 — Place the translucent underglaze colors in separate spots on a glazed tile and condition each one to a creamy consistency. Use a silk sponge to apply each color, as follows: Pick up the color on a small portion of the sponge and remove the excess by pouncing the sponge onto newsprint or paper toweling, then sparingly sponge it onto the greenware through the opening
Continued on page 54

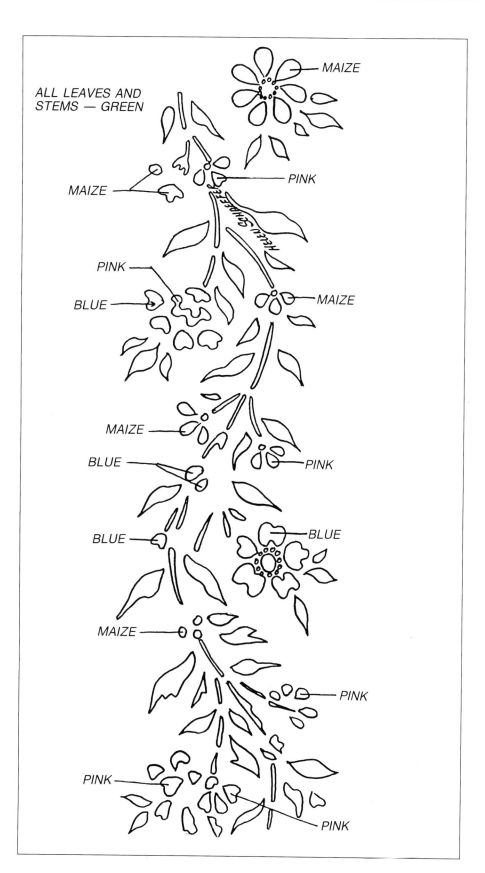

ALL LEAVES AND STEMS — GREEN

MAIZE

MAIZE

PINK

PINK

BLUE

MAIZE

MAIZE

BLUE

PINK

BLUE

BLUE

MAIZE

PINK

PINK

PINK

23

Satsuma Tea Service

Technique — Specialty enamel-type glaze and fired metallic

Satsuma ware originated in Japan with the coming of Korean potters in 1598 to the Satsuma Province. Among the best known of the Satsumas is the light golden cream color porcelain with decoration similar to that on the pictured pieces. This project makes use of a specialty product which may be unfamiliar to many ceramists. These enamel-type glazes are quite versatile, but seem especially suited to Oriental designs such as this.

MATERIALS NEEDED FOR THIS PROJECT
- ☐ Suitable molds.
- ☐ Oriental Flesh porcelain slip.
- ☐ Cleaning tools.
- ☐ Nylon stocking material.
- ☐ Glazed tile and palette knife.
- ☐ Glazes — High-fire clear gloss and Sung Yellow, Oxblood, Ming Blue, and Tea Green specialty enamel-type.
- ☐ Glaze medium.
- ☐ Brushes — #2 and #4 round, glaze mop, and brush reserved for gold.
- ☐ High-fire kiln wash.
- ☐ Liquid bright gold.
- ☐ Pen for gold.

Step 1 — Pour the molds with Oriental Flesh porcelain slip. Remove the castings and allow them to dry slowly.

Step 2 — Carefully clean the porcelain greenware, taking special care with the lids and the spout of the teapot.

Step 3 — Apply a liberal coat of high-fire kiln wash to the rims of the teapot and sugar bowl and to the areas of the lids which will contact the pot and bowl.

Step 4 — With the lids in place, fire the tea set to cone 6.

Step 5 — Remove all traces of kiln wash from the pieces, then apply 2 coats of high-fire clear gloss glaze to the inside and outside of each one. Dryfoot all

pieces and then fire them to the maturing temperature of the glaze.

Step 6 — Sketch or trace the pattern onto the tea set pieces ("Stabilo" pencils available at office supply stores which write on paper, glass, plastic, and metal are very good for sketching on glazed ware; for tracing, Mylar film works very well).

Step 7 — Use the specialty enamel-type glazes as overglazes for this project and mix them as follows: Place a small amount of the glaze powder on a glazed tile. Make a small well in the center of the powder and add the glaze medium, using enough to obtain a mixture the consistency of heavy cream. Since this type of glaze product dries out quickly, mix and use only one color at a time.

Mixing the colors as directed, apply one heavy coat of each one to the indicated areas on each piece:

All leaves; Tea Green.
Blue flowers; Ming Blue.
Red flowers; Oxblood with Sung Yellow centers.
Yellow flower; Sung Yellow with Oxblood center.

Step 8 — Allow the pieces to dry, then fire them to cone 018.

Step 9 — Using a pen for gold and liquid bright gold, outline each entire design. Use a brush reserved for gold to apply liquid bright gold to the rim and border of each piece.

Step 10 — Fire the pieces to cone 018.

HELEN SCHRAEFFER

Sad-faced Willie

Technique — Dollmaking

We all love clowns, don't we? A pouty-faced fellow, with a gaily painted face is sure to be a favorite in your doll collection. If reproduction dolls have never tempted you to make a porcelain doll, maybe this fellow will introduce you to the wonderful world of dolls. He's a blue-eyed chap ready for a place in your heart.

MATERIALS NEEDED FOR THIS PROJECT

- [ ] Suitable doll mold.
- [ ] White porcelain slip.
- [ ] Small, sharp knife.
- [ ] Cleaning tools and 20mm eye sizer.
- [ ] Nylon stocking material.
- [ ] Cotton balls.
- [ ] #220 grit scrubber.
- [ ] China paints — Pompadour Red, Celeste Blue, Blood Red, Golden Yellow, Black matte and Black gloss.
- [ ] Brushing medium.
- [ ] Pen medium.
- [ ] Brushes — #6/0 liner, pointed round, and china mop.
- [ ] Palette knife.
- [ ] Eye wax and setting compound.
- [ ] 18mm round blue glass eyes.
- [ ] Composition body.
- [ ] Pate.
- [ ] Wig to complement costume.

Step 1 — Cast the head mold in White porcelain slip.

Step 2 — Allow the greenware to dry to the leather-hard stage, then use a small, sharp knife to cut out the eyes. Hold the knife at a 45 degree angle to bevel the insides of the eye sockets. Cut out the back of the head.

Allow the piece to dry thoroughly.

Step 3 — Carefully fettle the mold seam lines from the head. Smooth the seam areas by gently rubbing over them in a circular motion with nylon stocking material. Inspect the face for any imperfections and remove them with a cotton ball.

The cleaning process is vital to the success of this project. Any flaws left on the face will be exaggerated when the china paints are applied. NEVER use water when cleaning porcelain, as it can obliterate fine details, cause a grainy texture, or cause the fired porcelain to have a shiny appearance.

Step 4 — Cover a 20mm eye sizer with nylon stocking material and gently rotate it inside of the head in each eye opening to create the sockets which will contain the eyes. Because of the amount of shrinkage when the porcelain is fired, use an eye sizer two millimeters larger than the selected glass eyes.

When both eyes have been sized, smooth the outside rims with a dry bristle brush. Incise your name and the date on the back of the head where they can be seen.

Step 5 — Fire the doll head on a bed of silica sand to cone 6.

Step 6 — Use a #220 grit scrubber to smooth the head, paying special attention to the hard-to-reach areas of the mouth, nostrils, and ears. Scrub these areas with a worn toothbrush and kitchen cleanser to assure smoothness. Remember, the end results will reflect how carefully you have cleaned and smoothed the piece. Any remaining rough spots will "grab" and hold more color and give the piece a blotchy look.

Step 7 — Refer to the drawing for color placement when painting the face.

First Firing

Paint the areas around the eyes with Golden Yellow. Use Celeste Blue for the triangles above and to the sides of the eyes. Make the teardrop design on the nose and the lips Blood Red.

Fire the head to cone 018.

Second Firing

Mix equal parts of Black gloss and Black matte china paints and add a few drops of pen medium. Use a #6/0 liner brush and the Black mixture to stroke in the eyelashes. Add a black rim around the eye openings to set off Willie's blue eyes.

Apply another coat of Celeste Blue to the triangular areas and a second coat of Blood Red to the nose design and the lips.

Fire the piece to cone 018.

Third Firing

Sparingly oil the cheeks with brushing medium. Apply a little Pompadour Red and use a china mop brush to blend the color for a natural look. Use a small, pointed brush to apply light dots of the same color in the corner of each eye and in the nostrils.

Apply more color as needed to the blue and red areas.

Fire the head to cone 018.

Step 8 — Inspect the head and, if necessary, apply additional china paint and refire.

When the coloring of the head is to your liking, gently buff the piece with a worn #220 grit scrubber.

Step 9 — Apply eye-setting wax inside of the head to the beveled socket of each eye. Seat the eyes so that they are looking straight ahead. Mix a small quantity of eye-setting compound and carefully place it inside the head around the eyes to hold them securely in place.

Allow the compound to dry.

Step 10 — Securely fasten the head onto a composition body. Glue a pate to the head opening and fasten a suitable wig to the pate.

Dress the clown as you please and he will always be your special fellow.

Field Daisies and Queen Anne's Lace

Technique — Brushwork

The decoration on this piece is an airy summer design done with translucent underglaze colors and stand-up-type glaze on a rich brown porcelain background.

MATERIALS NEEDED FOR THIS PROJECT
☐ Suitable brown porcelain greenware vase.
☐ Cleaning tools.
☐ Nylon stocking material.
☐ Glazed tile and palette knife.
☐ Plastic mesh-type pot scrubber.
☐ Translucent underglaze colors — White, Lemon Drop, Maize, Rawhide, Cinnamon, Green Grape, Spruce Green, and Black.
☐ High-fire clear gloss glaze.
☐ White stand-up-type glaze.
☐ Brushes — #4 round, #10 square shader, #2 liner, and glaze mop.

Step 1 — Cast a suitable vase mold with Brown porcelain slip.

Step 2 — Allow the greenware to dry thoroughly, then smooth the mold seam lines and the rim, using nylon stocking material.

Step 3 — Sketch or trace the design onto the greenware.

Step 4 — Place some of each translucent underglaze color in a separate spot on a glazed tile or other palette and thin to a creamy consistency.

Fill in all of the leaves and stems with two coats of Green Grape. Using a #10 square shader brush, shade these leaves with Spruce Green along the bottoms and with a little Rawhide on the tops. Add some Lemon Drop to Green Grape and use the mixture on a #2 liner brush to add the leaf veins.

Step 5 — Load a #4 round brush with Lemon Drop and use it to stroke in the daisy petals. Pull each petal from its outer edge toward the center of the flower. Separate the petals by shading and detailing them with Maize. Make the centers of the top two daisies with Green Grape and detail them with Spruce Green. Stipple a small amount of Cinnamon around the base of each flower center and on the very top of each one. Do the center of the bottom daisy in two parts, making the top Green Grape detailed with Spruce Green and the bottom Rawhide stippled with Maize and Cinnamon.

Step 6 — Paint the moth's wings with three even coats of White translucent underglaze color. Use a #2 liner brush and Black to add the details to the insect.

Step 7 — Mix Green Grape and Spruce Green and use the mixture to paint the stems of the Queen Anne's lace. Shade the stems with pure Spruce Green.

To give the Queen Anne's lace its texture and airy look, use a plastic mesh-type pot scrubber. Place some White stand-up-type glaze on a glazed tile. Press a portion of the pot scrubber into the glaze and then "print" the

Continued on page 54

Waterlily Vase

Technique — Incising

The striking yet simple design on the pictured vase was inspired by a piece of Kutani porcelain. This is an excellent design on which to try your hand at incising.

MATERIALS NEEDED FOR THIS PROJECT
- [ ] Suitable leather-hard white porcelain greenware vase.
- [ ] Sgraffitto tool.
- [ ] Cleaning tools.
- [ ] Nylon stocking material.
- [ ] Glazes — Cloud Pink, Gold Float, and clear gloss.
- [ ] Brushes — #4 round, #4 liner, and glaze mop.
- [ ] Non-firing gold marker.

Step 1 — Cast the vase mold with white porcelain slip, allowing the casting to become slightly thicker than is usual. The extra thickness adds strength for incising.

Step 2 — Gently sketch or trace the design onto the leather-hard greenware, then use a sgraffito tool to carefully incise the design outlines rather deeply into the ware.

Step 3 — Allow the vase to dry thoroughly. Use nylon stocking material to smooth out the mold seam lines and the rim. Smooth any rough incised line edges with a semi-stiff brush.

Step 4 — Fire the vase to the temperature recommended for your particular porcelain.

Step 5 — Apply 3 coats of Gold Float glaze to the leaves and stems of the design, allowing drying time between coats. Fill in the flower petals with 3 coats of Cloud Pink glaze. Pour glaze the inside of the vase with clear gloss glaze and apply 2 coats to the remaining bisque areas of the outside, being careful to avoid the incised lines. If any glaze should get into the lines, clean it out.

Step 6 — Dryfoot the piece and fire it to the temperature recommended by the glaze manufacturer.

Step 7 — Use a non-firing gold marker to add gold to the incised lines.

(NOTE: If the green glaze you selected is compatible with firing gold, liquid bright gold could be used in place of the marker. The vase should then be fired to cone 018.)

HELEN SCHAEFFER

Floral Decanter

Technique — Underglaze brushwork

If you enjoy adding the life and dimension of shading to your painting, then this project should give you hours of enjoyment.

MATERIALS NEEDED FOR THIS PROJECT

- ☐ Suitable white porcelain greenware.
- ☐ Cleaning tools.
- ☐ Nylon stocking material.
- ☐ Glazed tile and palette knife.
- ☐ Regular underglaze colors —White, Celery, and Watercress.
- ☐ Translucent underglaze colors — White, Lemondrop Yellow, Maize, Rawhide, French Lilac, Wisteria, Heavenly Blue, Spruce Green, and Black.
- ☐ Glazes — Thistle and high-fire clear gloss.
- ☐ Brushes — #'s 4 and 6 rounds, #10 square shader, #2 liner, and glaze mop.
- ☐ High-fire kiln wash.

Step 1 — Cast the decanter and stopper with white porcelain slip.

Step 2 — Allow the greenware to dry thoroughly, then carefully clean it with nylon stocking material. Check to be sure that the lid fits correctly.

Step 3 — Sketch or trace the pattern onto the decanter.

Step 4 — Block in the large areas of the design, applying 3 smooth coats of regular underglaze color to each one as follows:

Butterfly, flowers, and insects; White.

Long, slender leaves; Celery.

All remaining leaves and stems; Watercress.

Step 5 — Place some of each translucent underglaze color in a separate spot on the glazed tile and thin it to a creamy consistency.

Corner load a #10 square shader brush with Spruce Green. Shade this color along the bottom side of each long, slender leaf, referring to the photo for color placement. Shade the same areas on several leaves with Rawhide. Paint the long leaf veins and outlines with Spruce Green, using a #2 liner brush.

Step 6 — Shade the large, Watercress-colored leaves, using the square shader brush and Spruce Green along the bottom sides and Rawhide along the top side of each one. Mix a small amount of Black translucent underglaze color into some Spruce Green and, using the #2 liner brush, add the veins and outlines to these leaves.

Step 7 — Separate the petals of the flowers by shading them with the #10 brush and French Lilac translucent underglaze color. Shade around the top edge of each petal with Lemondrop Yellow. For the detail lines on the flowers, use the #2 liner brush loaded with Wisteria translucent underglaze color. Add some French Lilac lines to the flowers and use the same color for the outlines.

Stipple very dry Maize translucent underglaze color around the centers of the flowers, using a round brush. Stipple Black around each center.

Step 8 — Shade the butterfly, using the square shader brush and Maize translucent under-

Continued on page 54

33

Pierced Porcelain Candy Dish

Technique — Piercing

Many years ago I wrote an article on piercing a porcelain piece for *CERAMIC Arts & Crafts* magazine. Folks still ask for information on the technique, so I knew that it had to be included here.

Much pierced work executed before the ware was fired was done in China during the Ming Dynasty (1368 to 1644). Such work was often called *Kuei Kung* or "demon's work," because of the almost supernatural skill it was supposed to have required. Fear not! supernatural skill is not a requirement; one need only possess patience.

MATERIALS NEEDED FOR THIS PROJECT

- ☐ Suitable porcelain greenware.
- ☐ Small, sharp knife.
- ☐ Silk sponge.
- ☐ Cleaning tools.
- ☐ High-fire kiln wash.
- ☐ High-fire gloss glaze.
- ☐ Glazed tile.
- ☐ China paints — Royal Violet, Blue Violet, Golden Yellow, Black, Auburn Brown, Light Blue, Blossom Pink, Pompadour Red, Yellow Orange, Dark Brown, Yellow Green, Shading Green, Dark Green, and Yellow Red.
- ☐ China paint medium.
- ☐ Liquid bright gold.
- ☐ Brushes — #'s 2 and 4 round sables, #2 liner, glaze mop, and brush reserved for gold.

Step 1 — Cast the candy dish with white porcelain slip, or have it cast at your favorite ceramics studio. Keep the greenware damp until you are ready to work on it.

Step 2 — Mentally plan a random pattern of small, irregular shapes over the entire surface of the jar and the lid. If desired, these shapes can be lightly indicated on the damp greenware with a blunt pencil.

Use a small, sharp knife to carefully cut out the irregularly shaped areas. Work with a light hand, since the porcelain clay structure is weakened as work progresses and breakage and/or sagging can occur. (I use my left hand to support the inside of the ware while doing the piercing with my right hand; left-handed individuals would reverse this procedure.) If any area of the piece appears to be getting soft as you are working, wait a few minutes until it becomes firm again before resuming the piercing operation. Gently and carefully, while the pieces are still damp, clean the cut edges and smooth the top rim with a damp brush and a small silk sponge.

Step 3 — Cast the flowers, leaves, and the butterfly in white porcelain slip. When the pieces release from the molds, smooth any rough edges with a damp brush. Attach these pieces to the lid in a pleasing arrangement, using porcelain slip as the adhesive. Allow the pieces to dry thoroughly.

Step 4 — Apply a coating of high-fire kiln wash to the top rim of the jar and to the underside of the lid which will contact the jar to prevent them from adhering together during the firing.

Fire the dish with the lid in place to cone 6. Use a stiff brush to scrub off the residue of kiln wash.

Step 5 — Apply two coats of high-fire clear glaze to the dish and lid, taking care to work the glaze under and around the pierced areas and the flowers, leaves, and butterfly. Dryfoot both the dish and the lid and fire them, separated, to cone 4.

Step 6 — Using a brush reserved for gold, apply liquid bright gold to the edges of the cutout areas of the dish and lid.

Fire the pieces, separated, to cone 017.

Step 7 — China paint the flowers, leaves, and the butterfly with thin washes of color, as follows:

Pansies — Royal Violet shaded with Blue Violet. Centers, Golden Yellow detailed with Black.

Dogwood — Yellow Brown centers detailed with Auburn Brown.

Blue flowers — Light Blue with Golden Yellow centers.

Pink flowers — Blossom Pink detailed with Pompadour Red.

Yellow flowers — Golden Yellow petals, Yellow Orange centers detailed with Dark Brown.

Leaves — Yellow Green with Shading Green and Auburn Brown.

Veins — Dark Green.

Butterfly — Golden Yellow wings with Black and Yellow Red markings.

Step 8 — Fire the dish and lid separated to cone 018. If additional color is needed for depth or shading, reapply the same colors and fire again to cone 018.

Autumn Friends

Technique — Adapting greenware and oil-base stains

This piece, which I call "Autumn Friends," was created by combining several pieces of porcelain greenware. Hand formed leaves serve to add a professional touch and to pull the grouping together.

Once you have tried this technique, use your imagination to combine other porcelain greenware shapes to make your own one-of-a-kind pieces.

MATERIALS NEEDED FOR THIS PROJECT
- ☐ Suitable white porcelain greenware.
- ☐ White porcelain modeling clay.
- ☐ Rolling pin.
- ☐ Plasticizer.
- ☐ Small, sharp craft knife.
- ☐ Silk sponge.
- ☐ Rubber scrubber.
- ☐ Glazed tile.
- ☐ Petroleum-base non-firing stains — Bamboo, Walnut, Redwood, Olive, Orange, Yellow Gold, Maple, Gray, and Black.
- ☐ Stain medium.
- ☐ Brushes — #'s 4 and 6 round, #2 liner, and deerfoot stippler.
- ☐ Soft, lintless cloth.
- ☐ Wooden base.

Step 1 — Cast all of the pieces with white porcelain slip.

While waiting until the molds are ready to open, make the leaves, as follows:

Add a small amount of plasticizer to some white porcelain modeling clay to make it pliable. Use the rolling pin to roll out the clay and cut from it seven oak leaves of various sizes. Incise the veins and smooth the edges of the leaves, then place them on a piece of moist flannel in a plastic container to keep them damp until you are ready to assemble the piece.

Step 2 — Open the stump mold and use the craft knife to cut out the bottom of the stump and an irregularly-shaped hole from which the owl will view the world. Remove the mold seam lines and any irregularities. Turn up and twist some of the leaves so they appear natural and attach them to the stump with porcelain slip. Clean the damp greenware acorns and attach them at the bases of the leaf groups. Set this assembled piece aside to dry thoroughly.

Step 3 — Remove the owl and squirrel from the molds and clean the pieces while they are damp, or allow them to dry and then clean them in the usual manner.

Step 4 — Fire the stump, owl, and squirrel, separated, to cone 6.

Step 5 — Use a fine grit rubber scrubber to carefully and thoroughly sand smooth all parts of the stump, owl, and squirrel. Remember, that any rough spots left on the bisque pieces will catch and hold color and prevent you from obtaining a smooth finish.

Step 6 — Place a small amount of Bamboo petroleum-base non-firing stain on a glazed tile and add to it a few drops of stain medium. Use a #6 round brush to apply this color to the entire outside and inside of the stump. Blot back the color with a piece of soft, lintless cloth, so that the coverage is even with highlights on the raised areas and deeper color in the crevices. Apply Walnut to the crevice and shadow areas of the stump, then blend this color into the Bamboo with the deerfoot stippler brush. In a similar manner, apply a small amount of Black at random for contrast. Apply tiny amounts of Redwood here and there for highlights on the stump.

Step 7 — Paint five of the leaves with Yellow Gold thinned with a small amount of medium. Shade these leaves with Olive and a small amount of Orange. Use Walnut for the details. Paint the remaining two leaves Yellow Gold and shade them with Orange and a bit of Walnut. Use Walnut for the veins.

Use Maple for the acorns and Walnut for their caps.

Step 8 — Mix a small amount of medium with some Gray stain and use it to paint the squirrel. Blend and shade some Maple here and there on the squirrel for a natural look. Make the eyes Walnut with Black pupils and his nose and whiskers Black. Add a sparkle to his eyes, by wiping a highlight from each one.

Step 9 — Antique the owl with Maple. If necessary, use a bit of mineral spirits on the soft cloth to remove more color from the smooth areas of the feathers. Paint the eyes Yellow Gold with Black pupils and detail the beak with Black. Wipe a highlight from each eye and on the beak for a natural look.

Step 10 — Glue the owl to the wood base, then place the stump over him so that he peers out of the hole.

Lilies on Blue Porcelain

Technique — Underglaze and overglaze

The calla lily is often used for Art Noveau-type decorating; in this project we will use it on a Wedgwood Blue porcelain background, adding gold for a dramatic effect.

MATERIALS NEEDED FOR THIS PROJECT

- ☐ Suitable Wedgwood Blue porcelain greenware.
- ☐ Cleaning tools.
- ☐ Nylon stocking material.
- ☐ Glazed tile and palette knife.
- ☐ Regular underglaze colors —White, Canary, and Meadow Green.
- ☐ Translucent underglaze colors — Yellow, Pink Lady, Rawhide, Heavenly Blue, and Spruce Green.
- ☐ Clear gloss glaze.
- ☐ Brushes — #'s 4 and 6 round, #2 liner, #10 square shader, and glaze mop.
- ☐ Liquid bright gold.
- ☐ Pen for gold.

Step 1 — Pour the vase mold with Wedgwood Blue porcelain slip. Remove the casting from the mold and allow it to dry thoroughly.

Step 2 — Carefully clean the porcelain greenware.

Step 3 — Sketch or trace the pattern onto the vase.

Step 4 — Apply 3 smooth coats of White regular underglaze color to both lilies and to the bud. Paint the leaves and stems with 3 even coats of Meadow Green and the stamens with 3 coats of Canary.

Step 5 — Place a small amount of Yellow translucent underglaze color on a glazed tile and condition it to a creamy consistency. Side load a #10 square shader brush with this color and shade the top petals of the lilies. In the same manner, add some Pink Lady highlights and use Heavenly Blue for shadows on the lilies and bud.

Step 6 — Shade the leaves and the stamens with Rawhide translucent underglaze color.

Step 7 — Fire the vase to cone 6.

Step 8 — Glaze the vase, inside and out, with clear gloss glaze. Remember to dryfoot the piece.

Step 9 — Fire the vase to the temperature recommended for the glaze you are using.

Step 10 — Fill a pen for gold with liquid bright gold and outline and detail the design. Cover the entire background of the piece with an allover pattern of squiggly lines (see the illustration).

Step 11 — Fire the vase to cone 017.

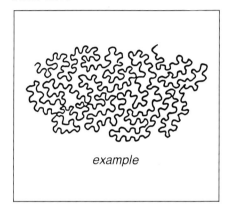

example

Blue Peonies

Technique — Brushwork

The tranquil attractiveness of this porcelain duck appeals to all who see it. The project used only three shades of color to achieve the serene beauty of the timeless design.

MATERIALS NEEDED FOR THIS PROJECT

☐ Suitable white porcelain greenware duck.
☐ Cleaning tools.
☐ Nylon stocking material.
☐ Glazed tile and palette knife.
☐ Translucent underglaze colors — Heavenly Blue, National Blue, and Black.
☐ Copenhagen glaze.
☐ Brushes — #'s 6 and 10 square shaders, #4 round, #2 liner, and glaze mop.

Step 1 — Pour the duck with white porcelain slip. When the casting is leather hard, remove it from the mold and position the head so that it is looking back over the wing. Be sure to make a small air hole in the bottom of the duck.

Step 2 — Allow the piece to dry thoroughly, then carefully clean it.

Step 3 — Sketch or trace the pattern onto the duck.

Step 4 — Condition Heavenly Blue translucent underglaze color to a creamy consistency on a glazed tile. Side load a square shader brush of suitable size with this color and apply it to the outer edges of all flowers, leaves, and stems.

Step 5 — In the same manner, apply National Blue to the undersides of all petals and leaves and wherever a natural shadow would be cast.

Step 6 — Add a small amount of Black to the National Blue and use this mixture on a #2 liner brush to add the details and outlines on the entire floral design. Use the same mixture to detail the duck's eyes and beak and to apply the brushstroke design on his sides and tail.

Step 7 — Fire the duck to cone 6.

Step 8 — Apply 3 even coats of Copenhagen glaze to the duck, being sure to dryfoot the bottom.

Step 9 — Fire the duck to the temperature recommended for the glaze you are using.

Cloisonne Peonies

Technique — Underglaze and overglaze

This easy-to-do cloisonne-type look is achieved by outlining and detailing a simple pattern with liquid bright gold. The end result is striking.

MATERIALS NEEDED FOR THIS PROJECT

☐ Suitable white porcelain greenware.
☐ Cleaning tools.
☐ Nylon stocking material.
☐ Glazed tile and palette knife.
☐ Regular underglaze colors —Lemon Chiffon, Valentine Pink, Jay Blue, Tropic Blue, Watercress, and Surf Green.
☐ Translucent underglaze colors — Orange, National Blue, and Spruce Green.
☐ Brushes —#'s 2 and 4 round, #10 square shader, #2 liner, glaze mop, and brush reserved for gold.
☐ Copenhagen glaze.
☐ Liquid bright gold.
☐ Crow quill pen.
☐ High-fire kiln wash.

Step 1 — Carefully clean the greenware, making certain that the lid fits loosely.

Step 2 — Sketch or trace the pattern onto the ware.

Step 3 — Fill in the indicated areas of the design with 3 smooth coats of regular underglaze color, as follows:

Large flowers — Petals, Valentine Pink; and centers, Lemon Chiffon, Tropic Blue, and Jay Blue.

Small flowers — Outer edges, Lemon Chiffon; and centers, Valentine Pink.

Large leaves — Watercress.

Small leaves — Surf Green, Jay Blue, and Tropic Blue (refer to photo for color placement).

Step 4 — Condition a small amount of Orange translucent underglaze color on a glazed tile. Use this color on a #10 shader brush to shade the Lemon Chiffon areas. In the same manner, shade the large leaves with Spruce Green.

Step 5 — Condition National Blue translucent underglaze color on the tile and use the #2 liner brush to detail and outline the entire design.

Step 6 — Apply a liberal coat of high-fire kiln wash to the top rim of the jar and to the bottom edge of the lid to prevent the lid from adhering to the jar during the firing.

Step 7 — Fire the jar with the lid in place to cone 6.

Step 8 — Use a stiff brush to remove the powdery residue of kiln wash from the jar rim and lid. Thoroughly wash the pieces to remove all traces of the kiln wash. Dry the pieces, then apply 3 smooth coats of Copenhagen glaze, being sure to dryfoot each piece.

Step 9 — Fire the jar and lid, separated, to the temperature recommended by the glaze manufacturer.

Step 10 — Fill a clean pen with liquid bright gold and add the details and outlines. Use a brush reserved for gold to gild the knob on the lid.

Step 11 — Fire the pieces, separated, to cone 017.

Floral Symmetry

Technique — Brushwork

This project features a repeat design in translucent underglaze colors. Once you have tried this method of decorating a sectioned piece, you will find it useful for many other porcelain greenware shapes.

MATERIALS NEEDED FOR THIS PROJECT
- [ ] Suitable white porcelain greenware.
- [ ] Cleaning tools.
- [ ] Nylon stocking material.
- [ ] Glazed tile and palette knife.
- [ ] Translucent underglaze colors — Yellow, Orange, Tan, Turquoise Blue, Light Green, Dark Green, and Red Brown.
- [ ] Yellow regular underglaze color.
- [ ] High-fire clear glaze.
- [ ] Brushes — #'s 3 and 5 round, #2 liner, and glaze mop.
- [ ] High-fire kiln wash.

Step 1 — Pour the jar and lid with white porcelain slip.

Step 2 — Allow the pieces to dry thoroughly, then carefully clean them. Be sure that the lid fits the jar loosely to allow for the thickness of the glaze to be applied later.

Step 3 — Apply 3 even coats
Continued on page 54

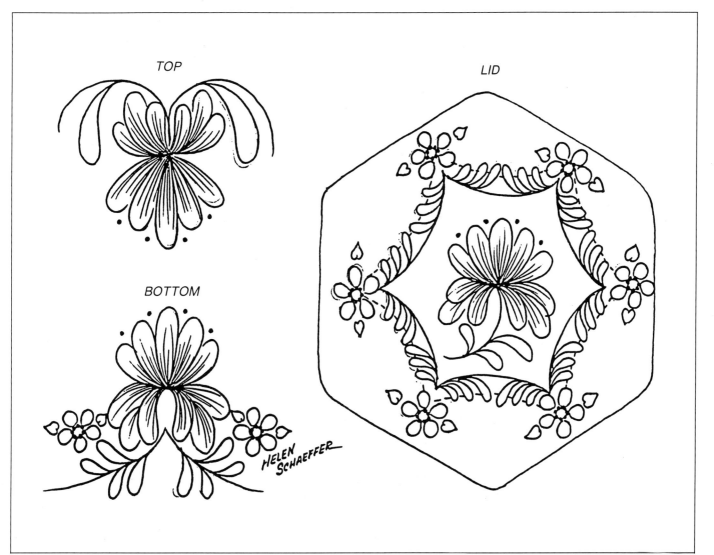

TOP

LID

BOTTOM

HELEN SCHAEFFER

Shimmering Pagoda

Technique — Overglaze

This striking accent piece was really very easy to produce. The design was influenced by Japanese Kutan porcelain. Do try decorating with fired metallics directly on porcelain bisque to see what a lovely soft glow they have when used in this manner.

Although this type of work is very dramatic on black porcelain as illustrated, you will find that liquid bright gold design work is lovely on any color of porcelain. I like the softness of the gold on the unglazed porcelain; however, the technique is also effective on glazed porcelain surfaces.

MATERIALS NEEDED FOR THIS PROJECT

- ☐ Suitable black porcelain greenware.
- ☐ Cleaning tools.
- ☐ Nylon stocking material.
- ☐ Glazed tile.
- ☐ Fine silk sponge.
- ☐ #220 grit scrubber.
- ☐ White dressmaker's pencil.
- ☐ Liquid bright gold.
- ☐ Brush and crow quill pen reserved for gold.
- ☐ High-fire kiln wash.

Step 1 — Pour the jar and lid with black porcelain slip.

Step 2 — Carefully clean the greenware, making sure that the lid fits loosely to allow for shrinkage.

Step 3 — Apply a liberal coat of high-fire kiln wash to the top rim of the jar and the bottom edge of the lid; the kiln wash will prevent the pieces from adhering to one another during firing.

Step 4 — Fire the jar with the lid in place to the temperature at which your particular porcelain

Continued on page 55

47

Black and White Floral

Technique — Specialty Glaze

Black and white is always a dramatic and attractive combination. While the design used here is striking on a black background, it would also be lovely on any other color of porcelain.

MATERIALS NEEDED FOR THIS PROJECT
- ☐ Suitable black porcelain greenware.
- ☐ Cleaning tools.
- ☐ Nylon stocking material.
- ☐ Glazed tile and palette knife.
- ☐ Translucent underglaze colors — White and Black.
- ☐ White stand-up-type glaze.
- ☐ Brushes — #6 round, #2 liner, and brush reserved for gold.
- ☐ #220 grit scrubber.
- ☐ Liquid bright gold.
- ☐ High-fire kiln wash.

Step 1 — Pour the pagoda jar and lid with black porcelain slip.

Step 2 — Carefully clean the greenware, using nylon stocking material. Be sure that the lid fits loosely to allow for shrinkage during the firing.

Step 3 — Sketch or trace the design onto the jar and the lid, repeating the pattern three times around the jar.

Step 4 — Condition White translucent underglaze color on a glazed tile to a creamy consistency. Use the #6 round brush to stroke in all of the flower petals and leaves. Paint the stems with the White color, using a #2 liner brush.

Step 5 — Apply the crosshatch design to the lid border and around the bottom of the jar with White.

Step 6 — Condition Black translucent underglaze color to a creamy consistency. Load the #2 liner brush with the thinned Black color and add the details

Continued on page 55

HELEN SCHAEFFER

Stylized Peonies

Technique — Incising

To the Chinese, the peony is a symbol of prosperity. The rather stylized peony design on this project was created to match a tapestry sofa in my living room. Because I was unable to find a red glaze to match the upholstery, I used red china paint for the flowers and borders.

MATERIALS NEEDED FOR THIS PROJECT
- ☐ Suitable white porcelain greenware.
- ☐ Sgraffito tool.
- ☐ Cleaning tools.
- ☐ Nylon stocking material.
- ☐ Glazed tile and palette knife.
- ☐ Black translucent underglaze color.
- ☐ Gloss glazes — Yellow, Evergreen, and clear.
- ☐ Blood Red china paint.
- ☐ China painting medium.
- ☐ Brushes — #'s 5 and 7 round, #2 liner, #10 square shader, and brush reserved for gold.

Continued on page 55

Dancing Butterflies

Technique — Brushwork

One of the Chinese symbols of married happiness is the butterfly. The romantic design on this vase was influenced by a beautiful pair of Chinese porcelains in the Smithsonian Institution in Washington, D.C.

**MATERIALS NEEDED
FOR THIS PROJECT**
☐ Suitable white porcelain greenware.
☐ Cleaning tools.
☐ Nylon stocking material.
☐ Glazed tile and palette knife.

☐ Translucent underglaze colors —Yellow, Orange, Tan, Red Brown, Lilac, Baby Blue, Turquoise Blue, Royal Blue, Chartreuse, Dark Green, White, and Black.

Continued on page 55

HELEN
SCHAEFFER

Stenciled Flowers

Continued from page 23

in the stencil.

Working as described above, pick up some Green Grape and stencil it onto the piece, repeating the stencil twice.

Step 5 — Cut out the sections of the stencil which are to produce the pink areas. Following the procedure as outlined in the previous step, sponge Pink Lady on all the pink flowers.

Step 6 — Follow the same procedure for the blue and orange areas of the design, cutting out the different areas of the stencil as you need them.

Step 7 — "Print" dots of color on the planter with a brush handle of suitable size.

Step 8 — Pick up some Heavenly Blue translucent underglaze color on the silk sponge and lightly pounce it around the top edge of the planter and the rim of the drip saucer.

Step 9 — Fire the pieces to cone 6.

Step 10 — Use a glaze mop brush to apply 2 smooth coats of high-fire clear gloss glaze to the pieces, being sure to dryfoot each one.

Allow the pieces to dry, then fire them to the recommended temperature.

Step 11 — Fill a pen reserved for gold with liquid bright gold and outline the entire design on the planter.

Step 12 — Fire the planter to cone 018.

Field Daisies and Queen Anne's Lace

Continued from page 29

glaze onto the Queen Anne's lace on the vase. Use the same technique to add a bit of Lemon

Drop translucent underglaze color to the Queen Anne's lace.

Step 9 — Fire the vase to the temperature recommended by the manufacturer of the porcelain you are using.

Step 10 — Pour high-fire clear gloss glaze into the vase and brush two coats of the same glaze onto the outside.

Dryfoot the piece and fire it to cone 4.

Floral Decanter

Continued from page 33

glaze color. Make the small spots on the wings with Heavenly Blue translucent underglaze color. Shade the insects with a bit of Lemondrop. Do all of the detailing on the butterfly and the insects with Black translucent underglaze color.

Step 9 — Apply a liberal coating of high-fire kiln wash to the top rim of the decanter and to the bottom portion of the stopper (the kiln wash will prevent the stopper from adhering to the decanter during the firing).

Step 10 — Fire the decanter with the stopper in place to the temperature recommended for your porcelain.

Step 11 — Use a stiff brush to remove the powdery residue of the kiln wash. Wash both pieces to remove any remaining traces of the kiln wash.

Pour glaze the inside of each piece with clear glaze. Apply 3 even coats of Thistle glaze to the side bands, neck, and base of the decanter and to the outside of the stopper. Cover the two flat design areas on the decanter with 2 coats of clear glaze.

Step 12 — Dryfoot the pieces and fire them, separated, to the temperature recommended by the glaze manufacturer.

Floral Symmetry

Continued from page 45

of Yellow regular underglaze color to the border areas of the jar and the lid.

Step 4 — Sketch or trace the design onto the ware, repeating the flower on each of the six panels of the jar and lid.

Step 5 — Condition Yellow and Orange translucent underglaze colors in separate spots on a glazed tile to a creamy consistency. Fully load a #5 round brush with Yellow and side load it with Orange. Use a pressure stroke to paint in each petal on the large flowers in the order indicated on the diagram. Reload the brush for each petal to be sure the color is strong enough. Detail these flowers with Tan translucent underglaze color and a #2 liner brush.

Step 6 — Condition Light Green and Dark Green translucent underglaze colors on a glazed tile. Load the #3 round brush with Light Green and side load it with Dark Green and paint the small leaves. In the same manner, paint the large leaves with the #5 round brush. Use a mixture of the two colors and a #2 liner brush to paint the stems.

Step 7 — Use a #3 round brush and Turquoise translucent underglaze color to paint the blue small flowers. Add yellow centers to these blossoms and detail each center with a ring of small Red Brown dots.

Step 8 — Apply a liberal coat of high-fire kiln wash to the top rim of the jar and the bottom edge of the lid; the kiln wash will prevent the pieces from adhering to one another during the firing.

Step 9 — Fire the jar with the lid in place to the temperature recommended for your porcelain.

Step 10 — Use a stiff brush to remove the powdery residue of kiln wash from the pieces. Wash both pieces to completely remove all traces of kiln wash. Thoroughly dry the pieces, then apply two liberal coats of high-fire clear glaze to each one, being sure to dryfoot both the jar and the lid.

Fire the pieces, separated, to the temperature recommended for the glaze you are using.

Shimmering Pagoda

Continued from page 47

matures.

Step 5 — Use a #220 grit scrubber to thoroughly polish all sides of the jar and lid. Adequate attention to this necessary detail will assure you a smooth surface on which to do the pen work.

Step 6 — Use a white dressmaker's pencil to lightly sketch the design onto the jar and the lid. The white pencil lines will show up very clearly on black porcelain and it is possible to do the gold work directly on top of them.

Step 7 — Use a crow quill pen filled with liquid bright gold to draw in the lines of the trees, bushes, and the pagoda. Use a small brush reserved for gold to do the solid gold areas. Place a minute amount of liquid bright gold on a glazed tile and use a silk sponge to lightly sponge it onto the mountains and hills. "Print" on the foreground dots with a brush handle dipped into the gold. Cover the knob on the lid with an even application of liquid bright gold.

Step 8 — Fire the jar and lid to cone 017.

Black and White Floral

Continued from page 49

to the flowers and leaves.

Step 7 — Apply dots of White stand-up-type glaze to the flower centers by "printing" them on with

a brush handle.

Step 8 — Apply a liberal coat of high fire kiln wash to the rim of the jar and the lid to prevent them from adhering to one another during the firing process.

Step 9 — With the lid in place, fire the jar to the temperature recommended for the porcelain you are using.

Step 10 — Thoroughly polish the jar and lid with a #220 grit scrubber. Wash the pieces to be certain that you have removed all kiln wash residue.

Step 11 — Using a brush reserved for gold, apply liquid bright gold to all of the raised flower centers.

Step 12 — Fire the jar and lid, separated, to cone 017.

Stylized Peonies

Continued from page 51

Step 1 — Pour the lamp base with white porcelain slip, allowing the casting to become a little thicker than is usual; the extra thickness is desired because of the incising to be done. Keep the greenware damp until you are ready to work on it.

Step 2 — Sketch or trace the pattern onto the leather-hard ware, repeating it on all four sides. Use a sgraffito tool to carefully incise the designs rather deeply into the lamp base greenware. Incise a border around each design.

Drill the necessary holes for wiring the piece as a lamp when it is finished.

Step 3 — Allow the piece to dry thoroughly, then use the nylon stocking material to smooth away all mold seam lines. Go over the incised lines with a stiff brush to smooth them.

Step 4 — Place some Black translucent underglaze color on a glazed tile and condition it to a creamy consistency. Use a #2 liner brush and the Black color to outline and detail each entire design.

Step 5 — Apply 3 smooth coats of the following gloss glazes to the indicated areas:

Yellow, flower centers; Evergreen, leaves and stems; and clear, flower petals and borders.

Step 6 — Fire the piece to cone 6.

Step 7 — Add china painting medium to some Blood Red china paint on a glazed tile and grind thoroughly. Apply an even coat of this color to all of the flower petals and to the borders of the lamp.

Step 8 — Fire the lamp base in a well-vented kiln to cone 018.

Step 9 — Inspect the china painted areas and, if necessary, apply another coat of the Red and refire to cone 018.

Repeat this process on the border until the color coverage meets your approval.

Step 10 — Using a brush reserved for gold, apply liquid bright gold to the detail lines of the flowers and leaves.

Step 11 — Fire the piece to cone 018.

Step 12 — Install the lamp parts.

Dancing Butterflies

Continued from page 53

☐ Brushes — #'s 3, 5 and 7 round, #8 square shader, and #2 liner.

Step 1 — Pour the vase with white porcelain slip.

Step 2 — Carefully clean the greenware in the usual manner for porcelain.

Step 3 — Sketch or trace the pattern onto the greenware.

Step 4 — Mix together equal parts of Turquoise and Chartreuse translucent underglaze colors on a glazed tile. Condition the mixture to a heavy creamy consistency. Load a #3 round brush with the mixture and stroke in one coat on the leaves which are to be blue green. Add a small amount of Tan and a wee bit of Red Brown to the mixture and paint the darker leaves in the design.

Corner load a #8 square shader brush with Chartreuse and, referring to the color photo for color placement, highlight some of the larger leaves.

Step 5 — Condition Tan color on the tile and use the #2 liner brush to apply it to the stems. Add some of the dark green mixture to the Tan color and detail the stems and paint in the leaf veins.

Step 6 — Paint the rock formation at the base of the vase with Baby Blue, then blend White and a little Tan into the center. Corner load the #8 square shader brush with Black and shade around the formation. Use a dry brush to pick up a small amount of Red Brown and lightly stipple it over the shadows of the formation. In the same manner, stipple a bit of Black over the same areas.

Step 7 — Apply White translucent underglaze color to the buds and to the White areas of the morning glories. Delicately shade the buds with Yellow.

Step 8 — Condition Baby Blue translucent underglaze color to a creamy consistency and apply it to the morning glories. Shade the petals with Royal Blue and detail the flowers and buds with Black and a #2 liner brush.

Step 9 — Paint the uppermost butterfly with White and shade the wings with a small amount of Lilac. Shade the wing areas next to the body with Yellow. Paint the body Yellow shaded with Orange.

Use Black and the #2 liner brush to add all of the detailing.

Step 10 — Paint the remaining butterfly's wings Yellow shaded with Orange. Make the body Baby Blue and do the detailing with Black.

Step 11 — Fire the vase to the maturing temperature recommended by the manufacturer of the porcelain.

Notes